ARROW TO THE HEART

Allan Havis

I0139943

BROADWAY PLAY PUBLISHING INC
New York
www.broadwayplaypublishing.com
info@broadwayplaypublishing.com

ARROW TO THE HEART
©2010 by Allan Havis

First printing: December 2010
I S B N: 978-0-88145-479-6

Book design: Marie Donovan
Typography/page layout: Adobe InDesign
Typeface: Palatino Linotype
Printed and bound in the U S A

ABOUT THE AUTHOR

The plays of Allan Havis have produced by San Diego Rep, Old Globe/Malashock Dance, Vox Nova, Seattle's A C T, Odyssey, Long Wharf, South Coast Rep, American Repertory Theater, Hartford Stage, Virginia Stage, W P A, Berkshire Theater Festival, Trapdoor Theater, Coral Gable's New Theater, Interact Theater, Philadelphia Theater Co, K P B S Radio, Vox Nova, and Rowholt Theater-Verlag (National German Radio). Commissions from San Diego Rep, England's Chichester Festival, Sundance, San Diego Rep, Ted Danson's Anasazi Productions, South Coast Rep, Mixed Blood, C S C Rep, Malashock Dance, Carolina Chamber Chorale, National Foundation for Jewish Culture, and University of California. Fifteen full length published plays, and also a Harper & Row novel *Albert the Astronomer*. He has edited two anthologies: *American Political Plays* (2001) University of Illinois Press and *American Political Plays After 9/11* (2010) Southern Illinois University Press. Also, his book on ninety years of cult cinema, *Cult Films: Taboo & Transgression*, (2008) University Press of America. In collaboration with renowned composer Anthony Davis, his play *Lilith* was re-imagined as an opera, premiered at U C San Diego's Conrad Prebys Concert Hall December 2009 and broadcasted on U C S D T V in 2010. Recipient of Guggenheim, Rockefeller, Kennedy Center/American Express, C B S, H B O,

National Endowment for the Arts Awards, San Diego Theater Critics Circle 2003 Outstanding New Play for NUEVO CALIFORNIA (co-written with Bernardo Solano) and San Diego's 2008 Patté Best Play award for THE TUTOR. He earned an M F A from Yale. He is provost of Thurgood Marshall College/University of California, San Diego and a professor of Theater in the M F A program.

ARROW TO THE HEART was first produced by
Vox Nova Theater, (Ruff Yeager, Producing Artistic
Director) in association with U C San Diego's Division
of Arts & Humanities, and the Department of Theater
& Dance, opening on 9 June 2010. The cast and creative
contributors were:

DAD ....Dale Morris
MOM .... Eva Barnes
SON .... Daniel Rubiano
4TH ACTOR... Robin Christ

Director...Ruff Yeager
Production stage manager .... Leighann Enos
Set & lighting design ....Gary Larson
Costume design ....Jessica John
Choreographer.. Miriam Cuperman
Assistant stage manager ....Asuka Anderson
Light board operator.. Emily Tracy
House manager .... John Martin

CHARACTERS

DAD, *late 50s or early 60s, educated, urbane, capable of vulnerable reveals*

MOM, *mid or late 50s, refined and reflective, resisting her greatest fears*

SON, *late 20s, nervous and thoughtful, fearing he will die from bad luck*

WOMAN, *mid 40s or 50s, quiet but active, always able to play other characters*

Twenty scenes (including prologue and final scene)

The play has been woven by chronological scenes, although the strict realism need not be maintained. For example, the WOMAN may actively coincide or engage with the family members during their few phone conversations. The WOMAN should not appear menacing, but she is assuming and she is often outside the interior drama in the manner of a stage manager.

Production note: The SON's monologues can be optional for production, including the prologue.

To Arthur & Molli Wagner for their special love,
support, and passion for theatre

Prologue

SON: I've a damaged memory like so many folks
have a damaged car, and yet I must try to remember
everything tonight...since the last twelve months of
my life I watched unthinkable things and I could not
accept what I witnessed. Memory is the closest thing
we have to preserving our souls—because prayer and
wishes fail. It's too much to say memory is timeless.
Memory is immortality. Poets have said it more
eloquently and warm hearted psychologists have
built entire practices on the notion. I've tried writing
memories down in a journal. Obsessively. I've tried
posting on a blog. I've tried talking to close friends.
I've tried talking to the best bartenders in town. Last
year my life felt like a plane spiraling out of control
moments from crashing. It was as though my ability to
remember became worse over time and today I cannot
distinguish memory from mourning. I came to believe
there was clairvoyance in our small world. It was as
though the telephone was the psychic link to a vast
matrix of lifelines and we often talk to the telephone as
if we believe we occupy the same room with the most
important person in our lives. And most evening calls
are from telemarketers. Alexander Graham Bell had no
idea what his invention has wrought, but I do not fault
Mister Bell. So the phone rings and rings and rings,
and we think about not answering it.

Scene One

(Phone rings. Perhaps a string quartet is heard. Phone rings louder as music fades out. DAD *and* SON *are in the same space, but have no eye contact)*

DAD: Hello.

SON: *Ça va?*

DAD: *Bon!*

SON: Had a croissant this morning, Pop?

DAD: Yeah, of course with chocolate filling. To hell with calories.

SON: What's your weight today?

DAD: Just a little above my bowling average. If you dress in blacks and vertical stripes, no one knows you're fat.

SON: You know I'm worried about you.

DAD: Well, late in the day I burn off the cellulite with hypertension worries. And you know, it kind of works if you stay in a sustained panic attack.

SON: Okay. I joined a gym and doing three visits per week.

DAD: And I can bench press fifty pounds—with both eyes closed.

SON: Sweet.

DAD: Wilton, our cranky neighbor down the street, has this old basset hound Trixie and called me over to watch his latest. He played Janis Joplin singing *Summertime*—you know that cut with the very long instrumental lead-in. As soon as his dog heard Janice hit the first three notes, he stood up and howled in tune with her. Kind of made a big impression. Wilton had me tape it for Animal Planet's funniest pet moments.

SON: That's good, Dad. I like *Animal Planet*.

DAD: So does Wilton. Wilton looks and sings just like the pooch. *(Pause)* When will you decide to help me in the business? Make some serious money.

SON: You ask this question every year.

DAD: I know and it's an offer you really can't refuse.

(DAD and SON laugh together.)

DAD: I'm the best Events Planner in the city and often the most affordable. My business is more than popping champagne and wearing party hats. My customers send me birthday cards, Nate. That is a measure of success.

SON: I'm not meant to be a businessman but you don't seem to get that through your thick head. You've bugged me since I was a teenager. I'm not your understudy. I'm not your sidekick. I've got my own life to lead. I want to be an educator.

DAD: You know I'm a salesman at heart, Nate. And I think you're from the same cloth. Teachers make peanuts

SON: Knock it off.

DAD: Okay, son.

SON: *(Takes some time to adjust his mood)* I got the grant from the Wallace Foundation. Readers Digest money, you know. It's a big fucking deal.

DAD: Congratulations!

SON: It's worth twenty thousand and complements my completed graduate Ed Studies. Frees me from teaching rich kids for three months. I can do summer school work for inner city kids. Send up fireworks now, Pop. Bells and whistles too.

DAD: Great news. I mean it. And I'll back off, Nate.
I don't like crowding you. It hasn't been easy lately.
I think you need to know...oh fuck, sit down, Nate.

SON: I am sitting down.

DAD: Mom had some unsettling news.

SON: She wrecked the car again?

DAD: No, it was the routine medical with her O B
G Y N. Her pap smear came back positive.

SON: What?

DAD: It's a little touchy right now. Thing is...false
positives are not uncommon and we're going to wait to
see before we sound all the alarms.

SON: Okay.

DAD: I'm telling you this so you understand what's
going on in her thoughts.

SON: So I can talk to her about this?

DAD: Well, only if she brings it up. You know very well
cervical cancer runs in her family.

SON: Cell phone reception sucks. What did you say?

DAD: I said Mom's family has a history of this. Let's
get off the roller coaster. Mom's not taking this very
well. False positives can occur when the gynecologist
fails to maintain properly sterilized swabs. The concern
is what the hell are these abnormal cells doing in her
cervix.

SON: Who's her gynecologist?

DAD: Doctor Campbell. He's tops, Nate. Really. I've
met him. *(Pause)* Campbell explained it very well.
Sometimes swabbing can pick up areas outside the
vaginal area—like the thighs. So bacteria on the skin
or from other patients falls onto the sterile swab.

SON: I got it.

DAD: So we'll know with more certainty in two weeks. She had a biopsy along with a second test.

SON: Shit.

DAD: To make matters worse, your Mom's friend Doris was recently diagnosed with stage two breast cancer.

SON: Should I fly home?

DAD: It's premature. Really. I'm just giving you a head's up. Mom's not here. She's out shopping. There's a big sale at Nordstrom's. I—

SON: That doesn't sound like Mom.

DAD: I know. She's not quite the same these last few day and I guess she'll do anything to keep her mind off her health. Besides, if she spend a lot, it will help the damn economy. Win Win.

SON: How is this affecting you?

DAD: I'm stoic. Like Rocky Balboa. *Rocky VI* was the best, Nate. You saw the film?

SON: I think I should fly home.

DAD: Whatever you feel you want to do.

SON: I'll ask if I can get away. I need to ask another teacher to cover for my fourth grade class.

DAD: Is that tricky?

SON: Depends on how long I'm away.

DAD: I'll buy your airline ticket if you want.

SON: Thanks.

DAD: And while you're in San Diego, you can give me a hand with some record keeping at the office.

SON: Record keeping?

DAD: My office has a few problems tracking inventory, invoicing … general crap…

SON: Sound like there's more going on.

DAD: Well, Nate, there is. I'm being audited by the IRS and that's as much fun as a root canal. The government's looking into four years of statements and receipts.

SON: Sorry.

DAD: Don't be. You didn't turn me in. Just give me a hand. Did yo know you get a "finder's bonus" if you blow the whistle on someone?

SON: Do you think Wilton turned you in or one of your competitors?

DAD: Who the hell knows, Nate.

SON: You really sound stressed and I know you got to watch your blood pressure

DAD: Don't worry about my numbers.

SON: I wish you weren't so stubborn.

DAD: I'm only stubborn with you, Nate. Get over it.

SON: Look Dad, I want to know how you can cope.

DAD: Badly. I see a therapist once a month, so don't worry.

SON: Bunny? She's not a therapist. She's a masseuse with horrendous logorrhea.

DAD: What the hell's logorrhea?

SON: Diarrhea of the mouth.

DAD: So she talks too much. She's got a license to practice.

SON: Come on. You need real support.

DAD: Support?

SON: Yeah.

DAD: From you and your idiotic Zen flashcards?

SON: Fuck off, will you please.

DAD: Don't give me the Buddhist philosophy, Nate. Your mom is too young for this torture and doesn't deserve it.

SON: Why the hell are you so pissed at me?

DAD: I don't know.

SON: About stuff from a year ago?

DAD: Nothing matters, Nate. You made many mistakes that I can't always forgive.

SON: I don't think my life's a mistake.

DAD: My business is a tangible asset and you had every reason to enrich yourself and help me at a critical time. But let's not rehash over the phone. I need you in my life and you know I love you very much. There...I said it. I love you. *(Pause)* So the plan is they will do second testing and keep things calm. *(Pause)* I feel so damnably stupid.

SON: Yeah, and maybe the doctor's at fault.

DAD: I really hope it's the doctor's error.

SON: Is it a flip of a coin, Dad?

DAD: Christ spinning on a coin.

SON: You think Mom'll be up for a call in the morning?

DAD: She'll want to hear your voice.

SON: Okay. I work most of tomorrow. I need to tell Cathy.

DAD: How is she?

SON: Fine. I gave her a project to keep her mind off marriage. I want her to think of a title for my book.

DAD: You're going to write a book?

SON: On new methods of social learning in grades K through five. It's with a university press.

DAD: Very serious.

SON: The book or my relationship?

DAD: Get some rest. You're tiring me out. We'll talk tomorrow.

SON: Bye, Dad.

(DAD *and* SON *hang up phones as a middle aged, well dressed* WOMAN *enters and finds a comfortable sitting position. She stares out silently neither telegraphing malice nor anything beatific. The men may notice her in a peripheral manner, but nothing more overt. String quartet is heard again as we set up for next scene. perhaps she takes out a cigarette, but she does not smoke.)*

(End of scene)

Scene Two

(The silent WOMAN *hands* MOM *the phone. The* SON *is dialing his cell phone. String quartet fades out.)*

MOM: Oh, I think I'm the big lottery winner of the month.

SON: Funny, Mom.

MOM: I know Dad told you the news.

SON: And I'm worried.

MOM: Yeah, baby, it's a bit of a spook show right now.

SON: Cathy sends her love.

MOM: Thanks and kisses back to her. Dad told me about the grant you just won. That's super, Nate.

SON: Do you talk to Doctor Campbell every day?

MOM: No. We just wait out the tests.

SON: I can fly out this weekend.

MOM: Don't bother.

SON: *(Tongue-tied)* You know we realize how serious... how awkward...hell... *(Pause)* We watched an old film on Turner Classics last night. Something you liked. Tony Curtis as Harry Houdini.

MOM: Oh, yeah. My old boyfriend Tony Curtis.

SON: It's a real cheesy film, Mom. And he dies in the Chinese Water Torture Cell which is factually untrue.

MOM: How did he die?

SON: Peritonitis thanks to a few punches in the stomach from a drunk college student. A show stunt gone bad.

MOM: You mean Houdini, not Curtis?

SON: Yeah, Mom.

MOM: Well, you live and learn. *(Pause)* My friend from my bridge club gave me the *Mamma Mia* D V D thinking that would cheer me up and actually it did. Normally I can't stand Meryl Streep but this was her best movie. She's so trashy she's absolutely brilliant. It's a three Kleenex flick. And I got all these frickin' Abba songs in my head. *(Pause)* Look , I did a little amateur research on the internet, Nate. You don't need a damn PhD.

SON: Checking the stats on false positives?

MOM: Ahuh. And postmenopausal gals are more likely to earn a false positive. Did Dad tell you I'm on anti-depressants?

SON: No.

MOM: Well, I'm telling you. And it has nothing to do with my thyroid.

SON: Since when?

MOM: Since I gave up drinking last summer. A A doesn't work for me and I don't like meeting in drafty church basements. I just found the right hypnotist. I'm sorry, Nate. I used to be a laugh riot with you over the phone—at least funnier than Joan Rivers—and this conversation is so damn morbid.

SON: Yeah, me too. I'm deeply sad and sorry.

MOM: And I had a dream last night that I had metastasized.

SON: Well, where's our magic wand Mom to ward off these bloody dreams?

MOM: Here comes your Dad and he's brought a magic potion called Starbuck's latté.

SON: You guys can sip some coffee. Tell Pop good morning. Tell him that Harry Houdini was Jewish and book smart even though folks thought he was Italian.

MOM: Your son says good morning.

SON: I'm glad you're both there.

MOM: Yeah. Well he's, he's...hold on, hold on.

DAD: Good morning, my favorite son.

SON: Hi.

DAD: Okay. Hey, about your hero talentless Conan O'Brien getting kicked off N B C?

(The silent WOMAN *takes the phone away from* DAD.*)*

(End of scene)

Monologue #1

SON: My Mom reads more books than anyone I know and she's storing all that data inside her little head—maybe the world's greatest computer is also inside her little head—and still she can be so expressive and simple in conversation that you just have to applaud and applaud this genius of modesty. She has the means to be the chief librarian of the universe, or maybe the den mother for all the distinguished faculty members at Chico State University—which is a joke because that was my safety school—I went to a much finer school. The letters my Mom and I exchanged during my time at college are all precious gems. She was provocative all the time and I was laughing my head off from her shenanigans. When I'm away for a long time, she's a great tease and not just a suburban Mom.

Scene Three

(Which becomes a meta-realistic scene with SON *meeting* MOM *in living room. This scene is a dream.)*

MOM: Put down the goddamn phone.

SON: Why?

MOM: Because I asked you to.

SON: Okay.

*(*SON *does and so does* MOM.*)*

MOM: Now walk over to me. Slowly.

*(*SON *does.)*

MOM: Thank you, Nate.

SON: I moved, you know.

MOM: I know.

SON: Can you guess the city?

MOM: Seattle? San Francisco? Santa Fe?

SON: Starts with the letter "D".

MOM: Duluth?

SON: Denver.

MOM: Are you happy now?

SON: No.

MOM: You need to be in a centered relationship.

SON: I am. With you.

MOM: Mother's don't count.

SON: Oh?

MOM: Not dying Moms, darling.

SON: Life support or not?

MOM: I've done it in my will. I've given legal papers to this doctor who looks like the little dwarf "Tattoo" from that 1980s show Fantasy Island . I don't want to be put on life support.

SON: Look at me, Mom.

MOM: Why?

SON: I'm standing right next to you, for Christsake. Look at me!

(MOM looks at SON and she smiles.)

MOM: I'd rather hear you. The pain is just unreal. So I said to Dad, maybe I'm terribly naïve but...

SON: Don't.

MOM: I could sit there and they'll jam me with the angel's morphine and I'm... *(Dreamy voice)* floating like a butterfly. Maybe you don't want to get here.

SON: Yeah I want to get there.

MOM: You want morphine, Nate? You know, when it rains it pours. Dad might go to prison because of this hellish audit. Or if he's lucky maybe a year of house detention with that wireless ankle bracelet. I asked Dad if you wanted to be here for this, or the service. We're talking real money.

SON: I'd rob a bank for you, Mom. Damn it. What's the point of acting poor?

(The silent WOMAN *moves a standing chair to center stage, as if to orchestrate* DAD's *entrance in the next moment. string quartet music is heard. Lights fade over* MOM *and we follow* DAD's *entrance to the prescribed chair. no phones are visible.)*

SON: What I told Mom is...I feel like now would be a good time to be there when...

DAD: You're acting scared like a rabbit.

SON: No, Dad.

DAD: I know you.

SON: You don't know me that well.

DAD: I fought in Vietnam. Where did you fight? Let me find out what I do about plane tickets.

SON: Yeah, the airlines have something called bereavement fares.

DAD: No problem about the money, Nate. I'll buy the damn tickets for you. And I'm going to beat this fucking audit.

SON: Okay.

DAD: You don't believe me?

SON: I do, Dad. I do. Chill out. I'll stay by the phone.

DAD: Okay.

SON: Just call me.

DAD: Nate, your mother died last night. Why are you so goddamn dumb?

(Silent WOMAN *unfolds knitting, yarn, needles and smiles*
DAD *leaves, while* SON *stays.* MOM *loses hospital robe.)*

Scene Four

(The WOMAN *now assumes the role of the* SON's AUNT
BETTY *who speaks with a rapid clip.)*

AUNT: I've read a splendid Anne Tyler novel. Twenty
years old at least. About a couple in the course of
a difficult day in their lives. The Breathing Lesson.
They live in Baltimore. On their way to a funeral. The
descriptions are brilliant, Nate. It isn't chick lit. *(Pause)*
It's great news about your Mom.

SON: I know, Aunt Betty.

AUNT: Wonderful news. Made my day. Aren't you
relieved?

SON: You bet.

AUNT: You know, more women get false positives
with breast cancer detection. So it's risky just going in
for tests. Don't know why Katie Couric televised her
colonoscopy. Maybe it helped her ratings. I'd prefer
looking at her face, Nate, don't you? I got the feeling
your Dad's not doing well...he's sending mixed signals
to all of us.

SON: Dad's being audited by the I R S. The shit's hit the
fan.

AUNT: Oh my God...

SON: I'm worried about him, to tell you the truth. He
has a weak heart and this is a lot of stress.

AUNT: He's got to relax now, Nate. Why don't you give
a couple of years of your working life? He can't run the
business alone anymore.

SON: I'll go crazy if I do that.

AUNT: You're stronger than you think, kiddo. That's why you should read the Ann Tyler book.

I think they made the book into a T V special with James Garner and Joanne Woodward. Yes, I did see it. Garner was good, but I don't know why they didn't cast Paul Newman? Really. She and Newman made the perfect Hollywood marriage, Nate. Didn't you like Paul Newman?

SON: Yeah, Aunt Betty.

AUNT: And I'm talking about the old Paul Newman. From *The Verdict* to *Road to Perdition*. Newman shines because he makes old age so sexy. Don't get me wrong. James Garner is thoroughly handsome at seventy. And look at Eastwood.

SON: I had a dream that Mom died from a morphine drip and the attending physician was getting us to sign a malpractice release form.

AUNT: Horrible dream, Nate.

SON: Right now Mom is healthier than Dad.

AUNT: That's right. Cholesterol, blood pressure, diabetes and he's still sneaking a ton of cigarettes.

SON: You nailed him?

AUNT: On the patio, yes. He hides cigarettes and sneaks out. Look in the flower pots, you'll find a ton of butts. I'm as upset as you are, darling. He's my brother.

SON: So will Mom's health scare wake Dad up?

AUNT: I'm a cynic, Nate. You know my answer. It's a congenital heart problem, but you'd never know from your father's behavior.

SON: I know. And his indifference to his health makes me feel like a damn hostage to a terrorist. Mom feels the same way.

AUNT: I know very well, Nate.SON: I'll work on him

AUNT: Good luck.

SON: Thanks for the call, Aunt Betty.

AUNT: Okay honey. How's Cathy?

SON: Fine. Not really. She's pissed at me.

AUNT: Why?

SON: We've been together over four years and she thinks I can't commit.

AUNT: You slept around a lot, Nate. You know what's out there by now.

SON: Do I? *(Pause)* I'll talk to you after I fly home. I got to see the folks.

AUNT: Bye, Nate.

(End of scene)

Scene Five

(WOMAN becomes 25 year-old, sexually attractive CATHY.)

(Café in Denver)

SON: Hello.

CATHY: It's me.

SON: I know.

CATHY: I love you.

SON: Hi.

CATHY: I wanted to tell you that.

SON: Well thanks.

CATHY: You're the one in my entire life I could say this to fully.

SON: Thanks…

CATHY: You are the one, Nate. Accept it. *(Pause)* He's special. You're special. The word today is special! Every time you read your fortune cookie, add the words...in bed.

SON: Cathy, listen.

CATHY: Your best friends want to surprise you... in bed. You will acquire a very big gift soon ... in bed.

SON: Cathy. There's a possibility I might have to go to California now.

CATHY: Nate!

SON: Listen.

CATHY: Don't do this to me. We haven't had quality time in over two months.

SON: Quality time?

CATHY: Quality time. Unrushed time. Good sex.

SON: I understand.

CATHY: Good.

SON: Cathy, come on. My Dad's going through a killer I R S audit. I got to help him out. There's a lot of irregularity and under reporting. I guess he took stupid liberties with his cash accounts. He's liable to face criminal charges.

CATHY: Oh my God.

SON: He's not very imaginative and I can help him out a little.

CATHY: What can you do to clean up his bookkeeping?

SON: It's dicey, I know. But I owe my father this. I can backdate invoices, polish some of his errors, and come forward about getting tuition loans from his business. He's going to pay a hefty penalty, that's certain.

CATHY: You didn't create his mess, Nate.

SON: Yeah right, but don't freak on me.

CATHY: I'm freaking, Nate.

SON: Honey, the good news is my Mom doesn't have cervical cancer. The rest of this crap is manageable, as awful as it seems. I know next week is your birthday and our four year anniversary. I know. I'll be back in time. I promise. I love you, Cathy.

(End of scene)

Monologue #2

SON: When I first met Cathy she wore very long, straight hair and kept her eyeglasses on all the time but she didn't need to wear glasses. I guess that was a disguise and I had to push hard to get past the disguise. She was so fucking beautiful and I felt like a troll next to her. She was open during our first date and when we kissed that night I felt that she was the most trusting soul in the world. When I first met Cathy she was taller and she knew I had a great case of nerves. She broke the ice and asked what book was in my hand and she seemed impressed that it was Thomas Mann. In her hand was a novel by Alice Sebold. Perhaps the most depressing book ever written and dumbest film ever made. The Lovely Bones. When I first met Cathy she could read every single thought that was lodged inside my skull. And I tried to read her lips and only understood monosyllables of luck, chance and circumstance. I took a chance and my feet felt heavier than boulders. She wore killer high heels, that's right.

Scene Six

(DAD *and* SON *are at the Miller house. A few days later)*

SON: I had a wonderful dream last night, Dad. We were in Tahiti. You, Mom, me. We were looking so good at this luxury hotel decked out in flamingos. We hired a yacht and a bird of paradise trailed behind. The weather was perfectly balmy and we didn't need jackets. Mom seemed so much younger, bronze tan, long wavy hair...it was so good I couldn't get out of bed. We were drinking very strong Passion Daiquiris.

DAD: You got to get a job, go to break a sweat, got to do what we call hard work. This philosophy stuff is just crappy cotton gauze. Right?

SON: Don't berate my academics, 'cause I worked my ass off. I earned my Masters degree at night and taught full time to pay for things.

DAD: If a tree falls in a forest, only the squirrels here it. Bishop Berkeley doesn't a blasted thing. Bring home the bacon, Nate. You get the reward if you do. It'll pay off. Everyone gets it, Nate.

SON: Business work means money, Dad. I get it. I'm not a top draw idiot. And I'm impressed that you know Bishop George Berkeley.

DAD: You need money. I need money. A Masters education is a nice trophy. Nate, listen, my business is taking a hit. I think we're all in a bad way since the economy tanked. If I could rob a bank and get away with it, the idea is too tempting. If I could push a magical, violent button and challenge my moral code for the gift of life, I would do that. I would wish the angel of death pass over our house and visit a distant stranger. Imagine that? I would wish for very compromising promises because I love your mother more now than ever before. I would deal with the devil

and sign his fine print contract. I bellyache about our
financial trouble too, still I know a lot of good people
carrying an interest only mortgage and their damn
monthly is about to triple. They'll lose their houses and
where the hell do they go, Nate? You know how this
kicks this country right inside the gut? We have the
crappiest health insurance for a modern nation and at
least twenty-five percent of America is not adequately
covered. One third of American kids are goddamn
fat. And we now live in a nation that allows crazies
with semi-automatic weapons attend a public visit by
the first black President. Fuck it. I worry about your
prospects and it's keeping me up late at night. You're
going to have to pay the piper.

SON: I'd rather just worry about today and not
tomorrow.

DAD: Isn't that an old Fleetwood Mac song?

SON: I'm not big on Fleetwood Mac.

DAD: So what is today, Radio Head or Sonic Youth?
And what about your buddy Paul?

SON: What about him?

DAD: What is he looking to do, Peace Corps or Teach
for America?

SON: Yeah. Teach.

DAD: He's still a close friend?

SON: Yes. He's the same as me.

DAD: A hundred percent academic?

SON: Exactly what- what I'm doing.

DAD: What the hell's wrong with my industry and
working the corporate landscape?

SON: Nothing.

DAD: What's toxic about my company? It's usually thriving. Companies and orgs big and small need event planning. Come work for me again. Try it for one Goddamn year.

SON: Right.

DAD: Yeah. I mean it. Summer vacation employment doesn't count, Nate.

SON: Right, Dad. Sign me up. We'll kill each other before the close of the fiscal.

DAD: I'll take that risk, Nate. Won't you too? Or do you think I'll just eat you for breakfast?

(End of scene)

Scene Seven

(Two weeks later. on the phone)

MOM: Hi Nate.

SON: Hi Mom. You don't sound very well.

MOM: I know.

SON: What's up?

MOM: Nate...your father's in the hospital.

SON: What?

MOM: He had a massive heart attack. Can you fly today?

SON: Of course. When did this happen?

MOM: This morning. I'm very frightened. Get on the first plane, O K?

SON: I'll be at the airport in twenty minutes.

MOM: Thanks, Nate. Call me when you arrive.

(End of scene)

Scene Eight

(Direct address to audience)

SON: I was lucky, got a direct flight to San Diego, made good time. Met Mom at the hospital. Dad was in critical condition and the doctors were sounding very pessimistic. We were at one of the best cardiology hospitals. This was Dad's second heart attack and nothing like his first. Apparently he suffered a great deal of damage to his heart and bypass surgery is not going to change the situation according to the chief surgeon Doctor Christmas and I was fixated on her name. Mom was putting on a brave front, but this event coming on the heels of her own medical issues has really knocked the hell out of her. That day in the hospital, we both felt he was going to die. And there was nothing we could do to prevent that fear. I stayed with my Mom for the rest of the week and miraculously, Dad pulled out danger.

(End of scene)

Scene Nine

(With the I R S AUDITOR at the Miller house. One week later)

AUDITOR: I'm so sorry about your father.

SON: Thanks for saying that.

AUDITOR: We were nearly done with the audit when you father took sick. I do need to complete the work and it does help if you can answer some of these questions.

SON: Over the years I have worked in the business.

AUDITOR: Yes, your father had mentioned that to me.

SON: My Dad had a few part time bookkeepers and they were never quite good at keeping things proper. Now that's to divert my Dad's responsibility with cash flow, errors in kind, and some of these missing receipts. I did draw some money from him for college and it was inappropriate if the funds came out of business accounts. But you got to realize that I'm back as a temp employee of the business during his disability period.

AUDITOR: That still doesn't impact or explain the spotty records of the last three years.

SON: What do you want? Kill him while he's in the I C U?

AUDITOR: No. Not at all.

SON: You have fifty million Americans avoiding paying taxes altogether, and a good man like my Dad gets tortured by the fucking I R S.

AUDITOR: We don't torture people, Mister Miller. We audit people. There's no comparison.

SON: You can say that to me and still call yourself a human being?

AUDITOR: *(Folding his binder to end the day)* I'll tell you what I R S can do at this delicate time in your family. We will only ask for back payments and interest from your father's business. There will be no jail time, Mister Miller, and that is a promise from me to you. We don't do this for everyone. And I'm as human as you.

(End of scene)

Scene Ten

(DAD on hospital bed while MOM visits. She kisses him)

MOM: You're looking much better, darling.

DAD: I put on some eye makeup, thank you, and I have a new comb-over—that is adorable.

MOM: Doctor Christmas said your chart's looking very good this week.

DAD: I know. It's corresponding with NASDAQ and Dow Jones. All arrows are going up.

MOM: Who brought you the flowers?

DAD: The girls from the office. They replenish the roses every few days so nothing seems to wilt in that titanic vase. Try lifting that vase.

MOM: Very nice.

DAD: And the Candy Heart Valentine You can almost feel cupid's arrow.

(Pause. With remote, DAD turns of hospital T V.)

DAD: I'm watching the news and it's unbelievable. The Polish President's plane crashes in Russia just as Poland forgives Russia for killing thousands of Polish soldiers in World War Two. This is not irony, but something more cosmic. The curse of the Polish. And it spares the Vatican a week of bad news about church pedophiles going free.

MOM: Let's not talk about the Vatican.

DAD: Okay. Let's talk about the German Pope.

MOM: Harry, please...

DAD: It's nice of Nate to come into the business.

MOM: I know.

DAD: It won't last.

MOM: I know.

DAD: He'll bail on me.

MOM: He has another career.

DAD: What side you do you take?

MOM: I don't take sides.

DAD: What are you, Switzerland?

MOM: Doctor Christmas says you'll be released in three days.

DAD: Connie?

MOM: Three days. When you come home, you cannot go back to work.

DAD: I know.

MOM: For good. You're going on disability. If you go back to work, it will kill you, Harry.

(End of scene)

Monologue #3

SON: Most kids go out with their Dads and they throw a baseball or a football or a frisbie, you know, and they go to games, or they go camping or fishing, and they might go to Monster Trucks or NASCAR, but really, we didn't do any of that shit and it's funny to think about what you miss twenty years ago when it can't change the picture today, no way no how. I think my Dad just dragged my ass to business conventions and promotional events which probably drove me out of my fucking mind before the age of thirteen. So maybe it's residual anger and maybe it's just a comic memory, and maybe I'm envious of all the boys who roughed it up with the Dads in the sandbox of time. And am I going to be a better Dad for knowing what the hell I know?

Scene Eleven

(At the fortune teller, the SON *seeks insight at the table with a bright red table cloth. The* WOMAN *dons a scarf around her head and she anoints the air with a scented oil spray. She signals for the* SON *to be absolutely silent while she lights three candles. The* SEER *finishes the ritual by humming a melody that sounds remote and eastern European.)*

SEER: Why are you here?

SON: A friend recommended that I see you.

SEER: What is her name?

SON: Sylvia.

SEER: I like Sylvia very much. Do you want me to read from the cards?

SON: What else do you do?

SEER: I can read your palms. I can feel the bumps on your head. I can read the cards.

SON: What do you do with Sylvia?

SEER: She prefers the tarot cards.

SON: Okay with me.

SEER: Is this your first time? Your life is in crisis? Is it your mother? I think I know. What is your name?

SON: Nathan Miller.

SEER: Are you Jewish? Don't be shy. *(She flips over 8 cards in plain sight.)* Pick out three cards that appeal to you. Some of the cards have pictures.

(SON does and SEER spreads the pack out.)

SEER: You know yourself very well. Maybe you had some emotional illness some years ago. Many people do in their twenties. And maybe your pain was a tool to reach spiritual epiphanies. Maybe you learned the greatest lessons of life at a tender age. Let's count out the cards. Count with me. We will stop at twelve. If your hand trembles, not to feel embarrassed. Some people who touch the cards feel immense heat. Others feel the stinging cold slap of dry ice.

SON: The cards are so damn cold.

SEER: Good. You can feel the molten winter earth under the snow.

SON: It's time for me to go.

SEER: Keep eyes close but rely on your hands. Today you are a young boy. I sense the lie and that is unhelpful to you. And little boys really hate to lie. Look at me. Do you need to be untruthful to me? Do you know you wear a mask? Handsome or grotesque? Do you know when the mask slips a hairline off its mark? Shall I be the judge or do you want me to be courteous? Don't you wish to be free of this weight? Your father isn't the culprit. I know you love him. He loves you unconditionally. I'm making you cry. He has money you don't want.

SON: Not true.

SEER: *(Laughing)* Or you want money that he doesn't have. Or the government wants his money. It's all the same thing. The cosmos is not connecting for you and your family. Still you don't know what to do and why you don't have much sex anymore. What is this about, Nate? I can call you that, yes? Your father was sick and now he's not allowed to work. That puts a strain on you. Am I right?

SON: Go on.

SEER: I think tomorrow will punish you for being unable to make a decision today. Such mild punishment, kindergarten punishment really. Are you able to make self-sacrifice? Do you get what I'm saying? I know you have human needs that go unnoticed by others close to you. Am I wrong? You now have a different notion about time. Once there was an ocean of time. There is a set limit. It's not mathematic. You were never invincible. Death is a poor video game. Expect no bonus round. Drugs mean nothing. Your Aunt reads the bible, did you know that? She doesn't tell a soul. She pretends to be agnostic. Tell her I know. You can pay me now, if you'd like. I have mercurial intuition, young man, and you make faces at my personal sadness. I lost a child to bone cancer. Would you have guessed that? Would you have asked me the right questions? Would you have felt the contour of my sorrow?

(End of scene)

Scene Twelve

(CATHY and SON are at a café.)

CATHY: What's up?

SON: Three days ago I went to a tarot card reader. She was sharp as tack.

CATHY: How much did you pay her?

SON: Cathy, I'm just saying she scored well. She knew a lot.

CATHY: That means you paid too much.

SON: I don't know if I should stay in Education Studies and commit to a teaching in public schools or go back to graduate school for philosophy.

CATHY: I thought you were itching to get to work with kids?

SON: I vacilate between two goals. I like philosophy Studies.

CATHY: Haven't you studied enough Bertrand Russell?

SON: I never liked Russell, Cathy.

CATHY: Wittgenstein?

SON: Yeah. Linguistics and metaphysics, darling.

CATHY: Every book you read pulls you away from real people, Nate.

SON: Lately I'm afraid of everyday people.

CATHY: I know.

SON: You act like you don't know.

CATHY: You're centered, Nate. You know yourself very well now. What you're most afraid of doing is going into your father's business.

SON: The business cannot survive without my father going back to work. He expects me to protect it from his competitors—during this hiatus. So maybe I'm indecisive because I really don't have a choice when everything's on the table.

CATHY: That's so idiotic to say.

SON: My Dad is allowed to live and maybe for a year or so. In the meantime, I have to think about what is best for the entire family. And the hell that I see in my Dad's face makes me refute all notions of a higher power. God is not a religious problem, Cathy. It's become a Doctor Phil problem. Don't you get it?

CATHY: No, I don't.

SON: God made Doctor Phil so fucking fat and bald and obnoxious. Ergo. If God exists, God is fallible. God is not evil, God is not all powerful. God is fallible.

That is the essence of modern day pain. God is like cable television. We think we need it. We think we're wired. We pick up premium cable. We think it costs too much. We never really use it but damn us if we cut the subscription. And when we call billing, they talk us out of cutting service. Right? *(Pause)* I hate the person in me that is crying out for God's hand.

CATHY: Who'd you talk to today?

SON: Mom this morning.

CATHY: Talked to your Dad?

SON: No. I talked to my mother.

CATHY: Uh huh?

SON: Why don't you kiss me anymore?

CATHY: Because you sound like Doctor Phil's son.

SON: Does he have a son?

CATHY: What if I'm pregnant, Nate?

SON: What?

CATHY: What if you have good news to tell your parents?

SON: Are you saying what you're saying?

CATHY: Yeah.

SON: We use contraceptives.

CATHY: Nothing works one hundred percent.

SON: So?

CATHY: So? How do you feel?

SON: I'm numb, Cathy.

CATHY: Get out of it, you dummy. I'm going to be a mother. You'll make a wonderful Papa.

SON: You thought all this out by yourself?

CATHY: I talked to my cousin. She's a shrink. She's very smart. I trust her, Nate. She's thinks I'm responsible enough to go forward. Whether you come or not.

SON: She said that?

CATHY: Yes, twice. On my voicemail too. You want to hear it?

SON: No.

CATHY: Do you want to get married?

SON: No. Yes. I don't know. My mind doesn't work that fast.

CATHY: Do you love me, Nate?

SON: I do. A lot. More than you think I do. You know I take medicine for depression. The quack doctors once thought I was bipolar. I was misdiagnosed and nearly hospitalized. Experimental treatment is for the birds. I watched a slew of old movies from the 1950s. Sam Fuller's *Shock Corridor*. I left the clinic. Far better to be bi-lingual than bipolar. Far better to be bi-sexual, for that matter. I don't know if I could ever make a decent father. If you gave me a few years to mature, Cathy, I might be a solid person, a real guy for you. Don't hate me please. My father's has only months to live, he doesn't know it yet, and I feel absurdly responsible for everything.

(End of scene)

Monologue #4

SON: I know I'm fighting something that is stronger than me and it's winning the battle. I thought that prayer was the best recourse, I thought I could dial in to some higher power, I thought that my life wasn't a fucking accident because there was a purpose to being here and being wide awake and functioning at a high level. Sometimes I had proof inside my heart that is all added up and good people are rewarded for doing good things. But at least two old friends had died with illnesses that could have been better managed. Sexual illness is quite a death warrant. And their deaths have a tinge or a sting, well, it is the feeling of helplessness and bitterness when young people just fall into their graves. And noble obituaries are for octogenarians. Old age is the stain of a criminal God. Because the vanity of being young is the euphoria of imagining that youth is your mirror. And every ancient tree knows that is just fucking solipsism.

Scene Thirteen

(SON's coat is wet as he enters the Miller home.)

SON: I was at the mall and it's still drizzling. What's up?

DAD: Nothing. All I know is that time is a cheap yardstick. Is that a mixed metaphor?

SON: Mom said they found some new concerns about your E K G.

DAD: Well, they did. It's a fucked up heart, Nate. There's congenital disease atop four other complications—I got a pinhole in my heart too—and I'm not a candidate for a quadruple bypass. I wouldn't survive the procedure. The doctors have been very forthright and capable. I can't blame them. A heart donor is the magic ticket, but the list for organs is staggering. There's no such thing as an artificial heart, son. And a synthetic replacement for the human heart remains one of the long-sought holy grails of modern medicine. I've read that somewhere, son.

SON: I'm impressed.

DAD: Don't be, I'm just a parrot on a perch.

SON: Do you believe in God?

DAD: I don't know and it doesn't seem to matter now.

SON: So you're sleeping a lot...

DAD: I can't walk much and I hate sleeping that much. You know that Jack Nicholson film, *The Bucket List*? Well, I have my Fuck It List. I can read it to you.

SON: Dad, I'll fill in for you at the business for the rest of the spring.

DAD: Don't bother.

SON: It's no bother. The audit's over. The penalties are manageable. I was persuasive. And I can get away from teaching for the rest of the term. The school understands. I can return in September.

DAD: Thanks, Nate. If you're sincere, this will help the morale at the office. My staff's ready to quit.

SON: I've talked to your staff. No one's going anywhere. Cathy said it was okay too and she'll come with me.

DAD: I think you're very lucky to have Cathy in your life.

SON: Yeah.

DAD: So marry her, you dummy, and be done with the headaches. It wasn't that different between your Mom and me. You will find there is purpose in life because you gave yourself fully to a gorgeous woman who loves you knowing all your faults. And forgive me for sounding like Yoda because and I continue to shrivel up I'm beginning to look like Yoda.

(End of scene)

Scene Fourteen

(The next day at the Miller home)

MOM: Did you have a fight?

SON: Just a small one.

MOM: What happened?

SON: She wants me to stop drinking.

MOM: Oh. Do you drink that much?

SON: I do. It's been worse because of all that's going on. You just don't see me drinking.

MOM: How bad is it now?

SON: I almost got a D U I last week. I was just under the legal limit.

MOM: Cathy knows all this?

SON: Yeah.

MOM: And that's why you're fighting?

SON: She think I can't handle responsibility on her terms. She says I have tunnel vision focused only on you and Dad.

MOM: Do you want me to speak to her for you?

SON: No. And I don't need a lawyer.

MOM: She listens to me.

SON: Stop it, please. *(Pause)* Mom, I got to tell you something first. *(Pause)* Don't make that face, listen… *(Pause)* I told Dad I'd help out resolving the business for as long as it takes. He believes me. He thanked me.

MOM: Were you B S-ing him?

SON: No. I think I meant it.

MOM: I hope you do mean it if you said it to him.

SON: So I really got to come through now.

MOM: It's generous of you, Nate.

SON: But I got to own up to something, Mom. Please.
I'll do everything that's possible to help but I never
really loved ad with my heart and soul. I don't know
why that is. It kills me for saying this out loud. I think
he knows and we cover what we know about each
other.

MOM: That's not true. Nate. You love him. You're all
messed up right now. And you both had some bad
incidents with each other over the years.

SON: When he was well he used to drive me nuts.

MOM: I know, Nate. But you do love him in your own
way.

SON: Okay.

MOM: Okay.

SON: And this crisis has inverted everything. *(Pause)*
I got very angry with him two years ago. I don't even
want to tell you how it got that bad. But it did and he
was cruel to me, even if he was thinking he was giving
me help. That's how he's built. You know that, Mom.
I'll never be equal to him. He created a business out
of thin air and he didn't finish college. He had years
of brilliance. He turned Events Planning into an art.
He rigs the game, Mom. Well, the point is, I started
to meditate a lot to get over it. But when I went into
very deep meditation I kept imagining Dad strapped
to a wood chair and I could punish him in the most
absolute way I know. I wished that he would get sick,
Mom. It's so creepy to say this now. But I got to tell
you this. You got to understand it. There was a stretch
of time I wanted him dead. I wanted him to get really
ill. And that he would just go away from exhaustion.
But you can see I fucked this up really badly.

MOM: You're not responsible for his heart, Nate. Stop this shit.

SON: I can't sleep well. It's running hard inside my thoughts.

MOM: Just turn it off. Tell me about Cathy.

SON: She's done it.

MOM: She's done what?

SON: You know. It. What she wanted. She figured out how to do it.

MOM: What? Stop speaking code. Pregnant?

SON: She's very pregnant, that's exactly it.

MOM: *Mazel tov. (With sweet humor)* Don't you use protection?

SON: Stop teasing.

MOM: I'm gonna be a grandma. I'll be a younger grandmother than my mother. Hatha yoga has made me so flexible.

SON: I'm not ready for this. I don't want to get married because of an obligation.

MOM: Nate, have you any idea how many marriages happened on earth because of pregnancy? Mine included. Nothing shameful. Nothing horrible. Maybe this is the gift from heaven that makes up for the present from hell?

(End of scene)

Scene Fifteen

(SON's *girlfriend* CATHY *visits* DAD *In the hospital. A few days later*)

CATHY: Hi Harry.

DAD: Cathy?

CATHY: Nate said it was fine to visit.

DAD: Nice to see you. It's been a while.

CATHY: You look good.

DAD: Do you think I'm too good looking for my height?

CATHY: Yeah, I do.

DAD: You can sit down if you want.

CATHY: No, I've been sitting all day.

DAD: Where's Nate?

CATHY: You know, we're having some spats.

DAD: Hell, I didn't know that. He's such a jerk.

CATHY: Yeah. How are you?

DAD: I'm hanging on, you know. Trying to make the insurance company pay through the nose

CATHY: I'll be at the house for the rest of the week. Your wife's been very nice to me.

DAD: Good.

CATHY: I know this is a very difficult time for you and the family and Nate's working around the clock to keep things together.

DAD: What are you trying to say?

CATHY: He's human and he's getting emotionally overwhelmed. I worry about when he's driving a car.

DAD: What should we do?

CATHY: Let him off the hook.

DAD: He's not on a hook, Cathy. Nate is free to do what he wants.

CATHY: I hope that's true. Harry please, this isn't the point of my visit. I'm just glad to see you're doing better. You are doing better, you know, I just ran into the doctor in the hall, Harry. She's saying you'll just have to change your life style and many people do exactly that.

DAD: I don't play golf and I don't fish. I'm a workaholic.

CATHY: I guess Nate wanted to find his free path.

DAD: He has. I'm not pulling any goddamn strings, Cathy. And maybe I won't see my next birthday. So what else can I say? Get married and have kids. Nate isn't a slacker, he's just a little confused. I'd say this to you if he's standing right next to you. I'm not pulling any strings.

(End of scene)

Scene Sixteen

(The silent WOMAN *puts on a telemarket phone headset, with Indian accent)*

AGENT: Bank of America Mastercard, this is Marsha Lynn.

SON: Hi. I got a problem

AGENT: Yes?

SON: My account has been frozen.

AGENT: What is your name?

SON: Nathan Miller.

AGENT: What is your account number please?

SON: 5478 9300 6602 2117.

AGENT: And your password?

SON: I don't know.

AGENT: And, what is your mother's maiden name?

SON: Goldman.

AGENT: And what are the last four numbers of your social security card?

SON: 1491.

AGENT: Yes, Mister Miller, how can I help you today?

SON: I just told you. My account's been frozen.

AGENT: There has been some suspicious activities in the last three days. Did you buy travel tickets on United Airlines for $387?

SON: Yes.

AGENT: And new tires from Discount Tires for $258?

SON: Yes.

AGENT: Are you aware that you have been delinquent on your last two payments, Mister Miller?

SON: I may have forgotten to make a payment—maybe—it's been a little crazy at home. My father's going to die very soon—terminal heart disease—and I need to...

AGENT: Unfortunately you have to make a final payment tomorrow or your account will be in serious trouble.

SON: But...

AGENT: You can speak to my supervisor, Mister Miller.

SON: I had a paying teaching job at a private elementary school. I am on contract to return to the school in September.

AGENT: I understand your frustration, Mister Miller.

SON: Then unfreeze my credit for now. I'm not in deep debt, don't you understand? I've had excellent payment history with MasterCard.

AGENT: That does not matter, sir.

SON: You're absolutely wrong. It should matter. I am your customer.

AGENT: Since you do not like my suggestion, I will now put on my supervisor.

SON: Okay.

AGENT: My supervisor will be coming in one more second or two. There are many calls ahead of us.

SON: Look, I'll make the payment tomorrow. This is not a problem. My father just had a massive heart attaché and won't live out the year.

AGENT: There are three more calls ahead. I can repeat this. Do you wish me to repeat this?

SON: Don't you understand what I'm saying?

AGENT: I understand. Yes. You will make the payment tomorrow.

SON: That's right. Just unfreeze the damn card today.

AGENT: We cannot until payment is received, Mister Miller.

SON: Am I talking to New Delhi, India?

AGENT: I am in Dallas, Texas.

SON: I don't believe you.

AGENT: You do not believe me?

SON: What's the Alamo?

AGENT: It is a car rental. I don't see that on your statement.

SON: Do you know *Debbie Does Dallas*?

AGENT: I do not know *Debbie Does Dallas*.

SON: Go screw yourself.

AGENT: *(Two loud clicks are heard)* Here is my supervisor. She will speak to you and I thank you for your six years of trust in Bank of America.

(End of scene)

Scene Seventeen

(MOM in living room.a few days later.)

SON: I think this Tea Party crap is the great undoing of America. *(He kisses MOM and turns of T V.)* Who pays for the fire department? Socialism? Look, after our hosing by the I R S, we should be starting our Tea Party chapter, it's just doesn't pan out that way.

MOM: Is Dad still sleeping?

SON: Yeah. He looks beautiful when he sleeps.

MOM: I know.

SON: He's not a member of the freakin' Tea Party?

MOM: No.

SON: But why the hell is he watching Fox News all the time?

MOM: It relaxes him.

SON: He used to watch C N N.

MOM: If Fox News is his worst vice, we're lucky.

SON: He's not sneaking cigarettes?

MOM: No.

SON: You search under the bed and in his secret cabinet?

MOM: Yes.

SON: So is he working with the nicotine patch?

MOM: No.

SON: Your hypnotist did a number on him?

MOM: No, your father cannot be hypnotized.

SON: I love Sundays at home with you. How are you doing?

MOM: I'm up and I'm down.

SON: Is that good or bad?

MOM: It's not bad, Nate. What's going on with Cathy?

SON: I told you. We're engaged. I bought a ring. We'll elope to Hawaii. She's on Cloud Nine.

MOM: Good. I hear the view is wonderful...on Cloud Nine.

SON: You like Cathy?

MOM: Stop asking me that, you clown. She's the finest woman you'll ever get.

SON: You only say that because she looks like you.

MOM: Nate, you'll appreciate marriage and being a parent quicker than a wink. And if you age prematurely, that's well worth the alchemy and loss of sleep.

SON: Splendidly worded, Mom!

MOM: And you'll grey before you know it.

SON: I read Susan Sontag. Cathy suggested the book.

MOM: Yeah.

SON: *Illness As A Metaphor*. You know the book.

MOM: Oh yeah. Thirty years ago.

SON: Right.

MOM: She had breast cancer.

SON: Sontag had to write about it. Otherwise it would drive anyone nuts.

MOM: I wish I could write. I would write my obituary.

SON: That is so damn macabre.

MOM: I'm trying to humor you, Nate. You have a black sense of humor.

SON: As well as you. You used to write essays, Mom.

MOM: And you remember that?

SON: I do.

MOM: Thank you.

SON: Sontag says that disease can define the age in which we live.

MOM: I know. She was a lesbian, Nate.

SON: T B once codified an entire generation of victims. Actually an entire century of fatally ill people. Not quite the notion of a plague. Still, AIDS marks substrata of victims. Cancer is our most modern disease and heart failure is the metaphor for our spiritual poverty. We've personality traits and destiny with these traits. We seek meaning with sentimentality. Sontag was fixated on the romantic idea...

MOM: The idea that disease expresses the hidden face of character. The totem face.

SON: Character is redefined to be the host of mortal disease—because it has not expressed itself. Illness is not simply a personality nor is it a lifestyle.

MOM: Yeah.

SON: "Illness is the night-side of life, a more onerous citizenship. Everyone who is born holds dual citizenship in the kingdom of the well and in the kingdom of the sick." Although we prefer the passport into the wellness, at times we must emigrate to the realm of illness. It's our personal stories about these awful experiences—about restitution and repair, about chaos and heroism—that best reveal what it's really like to travel through illness…together as a family.

MOM: You've committed Sontag to memory, Nate?

SON: And I've read too much Kierkegaard, Mom. Now there's a jolly Dane! Fear and Trembling and Sickness unto Death. He had one leg longer than the other.

MOM: And Sontag's funnier?

SON: Yeah.

MOM: Sontag slept with more celebrities than Kierkegaard, Nate. Don't revert to your fucking Kierkegaard days, for heaven's sake, you don't need to be more morose.

SON: Christ, Mom, I was never a monk.

MOM: Well I think you were, you dressed like a monk, and you were a very lonely one.

DAD: That's true. He was a dirty monk.

MOM: And how he'll soon be a father.

DAD: What?

MOM: You don't know?

DAD: Cathy?

MOM: You really don't know?

DAD: Nate doesn't talk to me with any clarity.

SON: Cathy's wish came true.

DAD: She's pregnant?

SON: Three months, Dad. I told you.

DAD: No, you didn't. Amazing. So a wedding on the calendar?

SON: Elopement. We'd rather spend money on the honeymoon.

MOM: Hawaii.

SON: Maui.

DAD: And we don't get to go, Connie? That doesn't seem fair.

MOM: Nate, do you want us to go with you?

DAD: Look, you can see the answer on his hangdog face!

SON: You had your honeymoon. I think I've earned mine.

DAD: You earn your honeymoon years after the wedding, Nate. Don't you know that? *(He drifts away into another room.)*

SON: Goddamn it. Why did he ever have to take up a fucking cigarette? What's the pleasure of lighting up? Of rolling the bitter acrid smoke off his tongue? For conversations on the patio? I used to hide the cigarettes, Mom.

MOM: I did too, Nate. When you were just a boy. Dad threatened to divorce me. Oh, he meant it. You bet. So he won and we lost.

SON: How are you going to be able to work? How the hell are you going to live without Dad?

MOM: I don't know. I can't think that far ahead.

SON: We can't be in denial.

MOM: Look. I'll meet someone else in due time. A bereavement group. Two of my friends go weekly.

SON: You'll never meet another man again., Mom. You'll never allow it.

(End of scene)

Monologue #5

SON: When I read up on the Jewish prayer called the mourner's Kaddish, it struck me that little is said about the departing soul. The prayer is mostly a tribute to God in Heaven and the coherent thought about magnification and sanctification of God. What is also stressed is eternity. And for a mathematician, there may not be a great difference between eternity and infinity. Both notions go on forever, but eternity marks time. So if we fail to mark time, we might escape the tyranny of time. So I know I might succumb and learn the mourner's Kaddish and chant the solemn prayer in all the cascades of vernacular Aramaic phrasing and feel the rumblings under the stone floor of a Jerusalem temple before an earthquake hits. Just another way of saying, "Our Father, Who Art in Heaven, Hallowed Be Thy Name."

Scene Eighteen

(*Several weeks have passed.* MOM *Is in hospital room with* DR CHRISTMAS. DAD, *with oxygen tubing to nose, is asleep.*)

DR CHRISTMAS: I'm impressed with his willingness to work with us, Mrs Miller, and you've been very patient with the hospital. We wanted to be conservative with our approach knowing the dangers ahead. But at this juncture and I've had other surgeons review this situation, it seems we shouldn't proceed with any other invasive measure.

MOM: What are you saying then?

DR CHRISTMAS: I think we should monitor your husband over the next few weeks and make sure his pain is not discernible.

MOM: But then you're letting him deteriorate?

DR CHRISTMAS: No. We want to see his system respond.

MOM: I thought you were thinking of a heart transplant.

DR CHRISTMAS: It still is an option but timing is not in our favor.

MOM: How long does my husband have?

DR CHRISTMAS: I don't know, Mrs Miller. Maybe a few months.

MOM: No. No. No. You promised me....

DR CHRISTMAS: That was weeks ago and we misdiagnosed a very rare problem.

MOM: How can you misdiagnose my husband?

DR CHRISTMAS: I'm overstating things—we didn't anticipate another complication that wasn't valve related. His muscle tissues are severely damaged. Trust us to do the best we can, Mrs Miller. I like your husband so much. Please know I'm dedicated completely to his well being. If you like, I can discuss this fully with your son. He phones me daily if I don't see him in the room.

MOM: I'll tell Nate. Don't bother.

(End of scene)

Scene Nineteen

(The next day)

SON: I had a very candid talk with my Mom, Cathy.

CATHY: Oh?

SON: She's told me that I've hurt my Dad in quiet ways. I didn't know what that meant at first or why she's

telling me this now after all my help. Guilt trip curve
ball. She kind of laid into me without thinking what
the hell she was really saying. And because she was
so angry about hearing Doctor Christmas's forecast
today, I don't think she knew how hard she was hitting
me. I didn't argue with her, Cathy. I took it like I was
a glutton for punishment. I took it because I wanted to
trade places with my father. I took it because I know he
was deteriorating and losing his dignity. And dignity
was always important to Dad. He craved dignity more
than financial success. Dad would fight anyone to
maintain his proper dignity. But how the hell do you
fight a failing heart? Which is worse? Old age or the
I C U? It scares the hell out of me. You know what I
mean? His personal things will outlive him, and his
reason for dying is louder than my reason for living.
(Silence) I once had comfort in my heavy arms. What's
the use of praying, Cathy? Is there a higher power
that is following us on Twitter or Facebook? You don't
really pray. Why should I? What the hell is prayer?
Would it be like an informal, ongoing conversation—
with a God who knows my every thought—yet invites
me to beg for what I want. Is that comfort? Assuming
God exists, does God have a sense of humor? What
does God think of the movie *Benjamin Button*? Should
we start out in life in absolute decay and rejuvenate?
Christ, my Dad is only 61. What comes of it, self-
delusion? I feel like such a colossal asshole. What a
neglected, lonely planet we inhabit. Jump over the
moon, there's a universe of cold silence. I wish I could
get high on morphine. Really. I never felt this kind of
pain before. I would surrender to a super sized double
drip, my arms extended like a Calvin Klein "Jesus"
in cotton briefs, my bare feet crossed, and if stigmata
happens—what a wonderful piece of theatre that
would be. I'm a little confused, darling. I don't know
which is worse in the history of civilization. Death by

a congenital heart failure or by a common criminal
at your door. It's like that old classic by the Rolling
Stones—*The Midnight Rambler*. Maybe the best song
ever on the creeping killer in your own body
Did you hear about the midnight rambler
Well, honey, it's no rock 'n' roll show
Well, I'm a talkin' about the midnight gambler
Yeah, the one you never seen before

CATHY: I get it, Nate.

SON: Do you?

CATHY: Maybe I don't.

SON: I think Brian Jones has it good.

CATHY: Who's Brian Jones?

SON: One of the original Stones who died and went
to Rock and Roll Heaven back in 1969? He was set to
overdose but it was bloody murder by a member of the
band. Still, he did one better than Pete Best.

CATHY: Who's Pete Best?

SON: The lucky drummer before Ringo Starr, a Beatle
before they were the Beatles. 1962. The Quarrymen
from Liverpool. Pun on personal best. He bought the
wrong raffle ticket and lives a life of cosmic obscurity.
Was it a deal with the devil or just another practical
joke from God? Ringo bested Pete Best. What was in
Ringo's destiny to supplant poor Mr. Best? And what
fucked up, cosmic roulette wheel did Mr. Best spin to
land on big number zero?

(End of scene)

Final Scene

(The WOMAN *becomes* GRANDMA. *She approaches* DAD *and removes the hospital robe.* DAD *is naked, his back to the audience. A pin spot on his shoulders, while the stage goes black. we hear* SON's *voice from a distance.)*

SON: This is it. I would take a bullet in the head. Come on. Shoot. Dad had a stroke last night. Oh God. He's as gone as a person can be. He might as well be on life support—and his chest doesn't even rise when he breathes. I can't believe it. Doctor Christmas said he'll pass by the end of this weekend. Doctor Christmas, rise from the ground's manure. It's now a matter of hours. His entire life reduced to this. My Dad. Now I can say I really love you. And Mom is a total wreck. She's aged ten years in one week. Cathy's here. She's aged too, worried about the pregnancy.

(The WOMAN—*now a meta-theatrical* GRANDMA—*begins to speak slowly, lovingly.)*

GRANDMA: The woman becomes Grandma. She transforms nonchalantly and some may think this is a spiritual shift. The woman becomes Time. God is forgiving. God is loving. God is profound. *(Pause)* Others may see this as an action from the land of no return. A land called by other names. A land that we now occupy as we face a winter sun. Happily or not. Awake or terribly numb. In grief or in acceptance. We occupy each other. *(Pause)* Is it very cold? Is it hotter than a brick oven? Look around and see your neighbor in denial. Or in faith. Your neighbor next to you. Yes. And squeeze that person's hand. I implore you. Now. Take the moment. Grandma is never refused. I am the Grandma of this story and I am your Grandma tonight. I can survive my own child. My son is in this hospital bed and he senses I am here for him.

*(*GRANDMA *adjusts her scarf.* DAD *walks into shadow.)*

GRANDMA: And I called him last night because one day your husband said he was having trouble coughing up blood...while the morphine circulated down.

SON: Morphine is the handmaiden of the devil, Grandma.

GRANDMA: And so Harry Miller, suffering acute chest pains, asked for liquid morphine—the fleeting mercy of love. What Nate once called "Jesus inside a drip tube" —that's right Nate. Let's call things for what they are. God in a syringe. Dear angels up high, please take away her terrible pain. Oh sweet Jesus. We love the mystery we fail to see. Ice cream lush vanilla. The sweetest legal vanilla. Oh, how your father loved ice cream in summer. And a thick wide sugar wafer cone. *(Silence)* The magnificent wafer. *(Pause)* Yes, Nate, this is an enduring forgiveness. The next day he came out of his stroke and was talking to Connie and seemed one degree better except that they knew that if he was on borrowed minutes. Dear Jesus in heaven, it would be like Lazarus rising from the dead and losing the dear mad voices in his kaleidoscopic head. See the spinning colors, see her emotional pinwheel, see the final expression, the lingering, his last loving kiss to this very young son, Nate. And he will build a lasting cradle in memory to his Harry Miller.

(SON walks over to his father. He cries quietly and he caresses him. There are no more images of DAD in silhouette.)

END OF PLAY

www.ingramcontent.com/pod-product-compliance
Lightning Source LLC
Chambersburg PA
CBHW070029110426
42741CB00035B/2702